19.95

P'TAAH

TRANSMISSIONS
FROM THE PLEIADES

The Gift

CHANNELED BY JANI KING

TRIAD
PUBLISHERS PTY LTD

For information address:
TRIAD Publishers USA, Inc.
23623 N. Scottsdale Rd., # D-3 (146)
Scottsdale, AZ 85255, USA
Ph: (602) 585 4287
Fax: (602) 585 2871

Book Title:
THE GIFT
Transmissions From The Pleiades
AUTHOR:
P'taah, Channeled by Jani King
Book and cover design by Peter O. Erbe

National Library Of Australia: ISBN: 0 646 24800 6
Printed in the United States of America

International Distributors:
Australia: Gemcraft Books, 14 Duffy St., Burwood, Vic.3125
Ph: 03-8880111 Fax: 03-8880044
New Zealand: Peaceful Living Publications, P.O. Box 300, Tauranga, N.Z.
Ph: 07-571 8105 Fax: 07-571 8513
U.K: L.N. Fowler & Co. Ltd., 1201 High Rd., Chadwell Heath, Romford, Essex, RM6 4DH, U.K. Ph: 081-5972491 Fax: 081-598 2428
USA: Triad Publishers, 23623 N. Scottsdale Rd., Scottsdale, AZ 85255, USA. Ph: 602-585 4287 Fax: 602-585 2871

Triad publications aim at aiding and inspiring a spiritually unfolding humanity.

PUBLISHER'S NOTE

Whenever we are acquainted with profound thought the joyous and the troubled heart alike are lifted beyond the boundaries of time and space into the Eternal. Such is the nature and purpose of this book.

The reader, contemplating a thought in earnest and desiring clarification, shall quite naturally find the appropriate page to meet his quest.

ACKNOWLEDGMENTS

Putting this book together has been a rather wonderful experience for me and has afforded me to look at areas of my life and beliefs about my life that have been, to say the least, somewhat inhibiting.

P'taah is such a gift to me; I cannot imagine how my life would have been without him. Working with this material has also allowed me to look at other gifts in my life for which I truly give thanks.

I would like to give thanks to my father, Arthur King, for being the man he was and for always giving me the unstinting gift of his love.

To my lovely mother Constance: I thank you for being the wonderful, funny, loving and generous friend you have always been. We have truly had some incredible times together. I am so grateful that it is you who are my Mother.

I give thanks to my beautiful brothers, Barry and Murray and their families. I love you so much and words do not express how precious you are to me. You have all helped to shape me into the person I am still becoming.

The ease with which this book was created would not have been possible without the support and encouragement of my beloved husband, Mark Emil Laurie. Thank you, Darling. Thank you for being who you are. I love you.

Grateful thanks also to my publisher and dear friend, Peter Erbe, who looks after me and supports me at all times. To quote P'taah: There are still many adventures to come, Beloved!

To Brian Dennis Ferguson, who chose to leave us: thank you for being our friend. You are in our hearts.

Jani King
August 1995
Scottsdale, Arizona

We *will* do anything to bring you Home!

- P'TAAH -

These words are given forth as a gift to you, each one of you; You, who I love absolutely; You, who make my heart sing; You, who be a most wondrous aspect of who I AM.

These words are simply to remind you of what you really already know.

I will speak to you, in these pages to follow, about fourth density, or Oneness, and the fact of the Earth and all which exists upon and within Her coming into a collective time of transition. However, be aware that each of you is on your own journey. Each of you is the central Sun of your universe and that the transition is your indidvidual choice, to come to know who you are, NOW.

- P'taah -

THE GIFT

hat very tiny fragment of you, which yearns for enlightenment, which yearns to Come Home, is the very tiny fragment of you which does not know that you are already enlightened and already At Home within the Divinity called God I AM.

here is really only one question: Who am I?
There is really only one answer:
I am an extension of the Mind of Creation experiencing itself
in this dimension of perceived reality.

*Know that you create your reality absolutely.
Who you are is a grand and multi-dimensional Master of Creation,
creating all the excitement and dramatic scenarios of your life,
day-by-day, simply for the experience of it all.
You have co-created the circumstances of your own birthing,
your family, your race and socio-economic circumstances.
All of this you have created, each lifetime, so that you may garner
every experience available to humankind on this plane of reality.
The universe does not judge these experiences, however they may be.
They simply exist in the IS-NESS of now, and in every NOW you
may create whatever you desire.*

There is an idea within the mind of man
that there are Grand Teachers to come forth to teach wisdom,
to teach you to find your Divinity.
There is also the thought that you may go forth to other places and
other planets to be taught, in some future time, how to know who you
really are and how to 'fix' the maladies of your heart.
We tell you no one can teach you. You are already your own Grand
Teacher and are as divine as you will ever be. If you are looking to be
perfect at some future time, then it will always be in the future.
You only have now.

nity on your earth may occur only
when you will grant equality and validity to the diversity which
exists within your peoples. This does not mean that you must be in
agreement or that you should all be the same. It is to recognize that
each person, each idea is a unique flavour of the Mind of Creation.

s you have perceived yourself to be separate from
the All That Is, so you have created 'need'
to fill the void of separation.
As you allow yourself to recognize the God-Goddess of you and be
filled with the joy and peace of WHOLENESS, so you will discover
that you have no need at all; that the outward material and
emotional manifestations of your life will reflect, automatically,
that fullness, without any struggle or strain at all.

Oh my Dear One, how abundant you truly are.
Do you not realize that abundance is not something you must go out and find? It is who you ARE.
The abundance of your universe is within you.
It IS YOU.
The glorious expectancy of the dawn, with its shades of silver, pink and lavender, is yours. The fire of the sunset is the passion of your life. The song of the birds, which helps the trees to grow, is also the song of your soul. As you gaze out onto your world and give fervent thanks for this abundance, which is part of you; as you feel the joy of abundance fill your heart, how can you not show forth abundance in your day to day life? When you are in fear of lack, be still and be filled with the richness, excitement and abundance of BEING.

Relationships, no matter what kind,
are an outward picture for you to gauge the relationship
you have with aspects of you.
When your relationships are not harmonious, when you feel
threatened, diminished, betrayed, not enough, or abandoned,
it is simply that you are in a place of fear and have a need
to look at what you believe about who you are.
As you embrace the fear that you are not worthy of love, or loving, a
new attitude toward yourself emerges, and the tenor of your
relationships changes to reflect a new self-love.

Fear has come about in your forgetting who you are.
You have forgotten that who you really are
is an aspect of the God-Goddess expressing Itself, however that may
be, in the vibrancy of this reality. There is no such thing as releasing
fear or hiding from it. Fear is valid. There is nothing wrong with fear.
It is the polarity of LOVE. The way to transform fear is to step into
it, to embrace it. You may picture fear as the child within you who is
terrified of being unworthy of love, joy, abundance and laughter,
doomed to abandonment, dying of a broken heart.
As you hold the child to your heart, say:
'Beloved of my heart, I love you with every part of my being.
You are not alone. We live in a safe universe, you and I,
and together we are going home.'
Thusly, you transform the fear to LOVE.

What is God?
Rather you might ask yourself, 'What is not God?'
God-Goddess, the Mind of Creation, the All That IS, you may say is
another description of love, and that is the glue which holds the
multiverses together. Without this energy force,
this Light of Creation, there is no life, no existence.
Every cell, every molecule, every sub-atomic particle shines with its
own God-light. As you honour who you are as an embodiment of God-
light, how can you not honour every thing and every one in your
universe as a non-separate part of that same Light?

Universal Law:
What you resist persists.
This simply means that as you put forth energy in resistance the
universe, without judgement, will support you absolutely and will
give you more of what you are putting your energy into.

LOVE is simply another word for God-Goddess.
When you express love to others, you are expressing the God-Goddess of you. This is immediately recognized by the others, because it resonates to their own God-Goddess.
This LOVE is who you all really are.

our every action, every thought, every situation is your own creation. To deny this truth is to admit that you do not know who you are.

Let us speak to you of your pain, my Beloved.
Pain is resistance to feeling
and created from your judgement: your judgement of yourself,
your situation and of the co-creators of that situation.
Yet judgement is also a Divine attribute of your being.
It exists to show you WHERE you are and HOW you are NOW.
It is simply to align your judgement by acknowledging it,
allowing it, feeling it. Be still and feel.
Your judgement is now neutralized and your pain is transmuted.

*ou have created yourself here and now to take part
in the transformation of your world.
This transformation is a shift in consciousness not only of humanity,
but of the planet Herself and everything upon and within Her.
Sometimes you become afraid that in this shift you will lose those who
are dear to you who are perhaps not as consciously aware as you.
Beloved, we would remind you that this change is about LOVE,
and love is non-separation. You will lose nothing and no one.*

*our mission in life is simply to come to know
who you really are. Everything else is a game wherein you may
monitor your own progress. There is nothing to DO.
You exist in your absolute perfection every now moment.
You are an exquisite jewel of creation NOW, not when you have
changed all of the parts of you that you judge to be unlovable. You
want to do great deeds, to be of grand service to humanity, but we tell
you that the greatest service is to come into the realization that
simply by BEING in the love and honour of who you really are,
you change the consciousness of all humanity.
Thusly, you will light up your world.
Can there be a greater service?*

The diversity of teachings in your world
are understandably sometimes quite confusing for you.
There are so many stories of light entities and dark entities,
implants and conspiracies, rites and rituals, and do's and don'ts.
There are stories about the evils of man which you must atone for
and methodologies to which you must adhere in order to become
enlightened. The list could go on and on.
However, the truth is that you are your own power-sourceness.
You are a sovereign being. The enlightenment you seek is already
within you, as is the knowledge of the multi-verses. If you want to
give your power away, then it is your sovereign right to do so.
You have been doing it for eons. If anyone tells you: 'You can only do
it this way,' bless them and turn away. If what anyone tells you is
fear based, fear inducing, or in any way limited or limiting,
bless them and turn away.

There is no judgement in the universe apart from
that judgement you have about yourself.
Every time you sit in judgement of anyone or anything outside
yourself, it is really you whom you judge. There will never be a time
when you are called to a higher judgement.
Very often in your day-by-day life you find yourself in judgement,
then you judge the judgement. What a double bind!
Well, that is alright. Just remind yourself that judgement itself
is an attribute of divinity. It is your yardstick.
It is your monitor by which you may gauge your own beliefs
and fears in that now moment. Give thanks for this.
From the judgement you may grow.

eloved, your longing for the fourth dimension,
or Ascension, or any reality apart from this, is simply
the measure of your dissatisfaction with the NOW.
Until you can come to the joy and fulfillment of this life,
loving your exquisite planet, healing the anguished heart,
aligning the fears that keep you imprisoned, living in the excitement
and fullness of each moment without a past or a future,
this dimension is all you can know. There is no escape.
That is the dichotomy: As you live in the joy and harmony of this life
experience without desiring any other, you automatically create the
space to experience that expanded reality called fourth density,
called Ascension, called ONENESS.

ll of humanity was star-seeded. Many of you are quite
comfortable with that knowing at this time.
Indeed, many of you feel that you are not 'at home' on this planet
and feel a longing to return from whence you came.
Some of you consult seers and teachers to find out where 'home'
really is. I will tell you: Home is the place within you that knows
itself to be in non-separation from anyone anywhere. It does not
matter where you are from. It is not important. It will not help you.
It is another diversion to keep you away from feeling,
from examining your beliefs and fears.
You have created yourselves here in this time and place
to become all that you can be in this reality.
There is nothing else.

our ego was designed to be the sensor of exterior life.
You cannot get rid of it or sublimate it. Indeed, as you try to do so,
the old law of the universe which states: 'What you resist persists,'
will bring the ego into a stronger and stronger position.
Yet your ego is a most valuable aspect of you.
It is merely to bring it into balance.
When you find yourself heartily in defense of yourself,
know that the ego is in fear of the judgement of others. Just be still.
Go to the fear and embrace the child within you who is afraid.
Also, it is to remind yourself that what anyone thinks of you
is none of your business.

Life IS meant to be easy.
Your life is meant to be of love and laughter, abundance
and fulfillment. What keeps you from these things is your old
emotional baggage, your belief about reality, and your fear that you
are not worthy. Every time you find yourself in a struggle you are
in a place of fear. Each time you refuse to deal with an emotional
issue in the now moment you are adding to your emotional baggage.
If you will not examine your belief structures and fears and deal
with the emotions, you limit yourself to a most confining prison.
Each NOW is another opportunity for you
to choose how it may be for you.

The preoccupation with what is right or wrong for you to eat is not necessary. Your health is not dependent upon it. That which is the beingness of flora and fauna, in a way, is co-created by you and by the flora and fauna for your nourishment, both physical and spiritual. The nourishment is gained by you giving forth thanks for what is provided to the Spirit of that which is ingested. In the opening of your heart and giving thanks, you cause the enlightenment of the food, the enlightenment of the spiritual 'body' of the food, and in the giving forth of thanks you are also creating the enlightenment of your physical structure.

Dear One: Forgiveness is a concept of limitation.
Does this sound strange to you? Well you see, in the broader
sense of things, no one ever 'did' anything to you.
You create your own reality absolutely.
Everything in your life you have created, or co-created,
and you have done so for your greatest spiritual growth,
whether or not you accept it as such.
Understand that every situation is a learning process
for the benefit of all peoples concerned, to help you to grow
in love, honour, sovereignty and compassion.

The natural inclination of your consciousness
is to turn toward the spiritual truths which reflect the Divinity
you really are. The natural inclination of your physical body is to
shine forth with radiant health, reflecting the Divinity
which is the life force within every cell.
Every part of you yearns to bask in the light of that Divinity,
called love, in the same fashion that a flower turns irresistibly
to the light of the Sun.

here is no such thing as extraneous creation,
or parts of creation that should not be, or that do not fit into your
reality. If something exists it is as valid as anything else,
or it would have no existence.

Guilt, Beloved One, is simply a lesson not learned.
Yet you have always done the best you could
in the only way you knew how. There is no judgement.
As you come into this more unlimited way of thinking,
as you come to embrace the fears, align the judgements and
transmute the pain, you will find that guilt will simply fade away.
You will not need to repeat the lesson!

*You have a most amusing saying in your world:
'Time is what stops everything occurring at the same time.'
This is valid. You may say that when you are birthed,
you are birthed into a time-lock, and what you experience in that
time-lock are the separate events called life.
You may say that time is a referencing point.
Then you experience what you call death and after a period
of other-reality experience you may choose to come back to this
reality, in another time-lock for yet another 'life.'
However, in a more expanded sense, time is simply an illusion.
Outside of this space-time continuum all of the lifetimes occur
simultaneously, each in their own glorious NOW.*

It simply does not matter
who you were in your past lives, or what glorious or terrible
deeds you performed, or with whom.
The only importance in your life is NOW.
It does not matter what occurred in your life yesterday or last year.
Whatever has occurred which is not aligned will be presented to you
and re-presented continually until you do align it.
It does not even matter what the 'story' of external events consists
of. You will notice that what will be re-occurring, no matter
what the story, will be the same FEELING.
As you go to the feeling, in allowance and embracement of the fears,
in the NOW moment you effect the change into alignment, not only
in this life, but in what you call your past and your future lives,
as all of the lifetimes are occurring simultaneously.

Love is the Alpha and Omega of your life.
Without it you cannot survive. Love is what fills the empty space
within you. As you become filled with the love of who you are,
in the knowing that you are an aspect of the God-Goddess,
so you radiate that love to all about you.
From this place of being, all that you will be able to perceive will be
the reflection of that love shining back at you.
Oh my Beloved, what wondrousness indeed!

It is time for you to learn to listen
to the knowing within you. When you find yourself in a muddle,
simply be still and ask from the God-Goddess of your own being,
to allow the wisdom and knowing to float into your consciousness.
Sometimes you invalidate your knowing because the answers do not
seem to make sense to you, or indeed, the answer is not the one
the ego wants to hear. It is to remember that your logical conscious
mind is most often not aware of the larger scheme of things, whereas
the greater part of who you are knows all of the probabilities,
and indeed, knows that which will be of most benefit to you.

o forth and do what makes your heart sing.
Please note that we do say 'heart', not 'ego'. You will find that simply
to gratify the ego will not bring you the fulfillment you desire,
nor will it fill the emptiness within you. Sometimes it is difficult
for you to know the difference between heart and ego.
That which is of the heart is that which is of benefit to all people
concerned in a decision. How do you know what is a benefit
when you do not have an overview?
Simply be still and ask yourself, then listen to the feeling.
The feeling of peace and comfort is your answer.

ngels and Guides are valid. However, know that the greater
spiritual beingness of you occupies all of the dimensions
simultaneously. At another level you are also angels and guides.
Therefore, it is of utmost benefit if you will understand that it is,
in that place of non-separation, all part of your own soul energy.
Instead of calling on an outside authority, call upon the unlimited,
eternal I AM. In this fashion you strengthen your own
power sourceness.

implicity, Dear One, that is the key. Keep it Simple!
If you feel joyous then go with the flow of it.
If it is not harmonious, be still. Examine the beliefs you have
about the situation. Go to the feeling, embrace the fear
and transmute the pain. Everything else is just a story.

s you grow in awareness and expand your consciousness
you will find that your view of your world also expands.
As you view the dramas and pain and anguish
of your brothers and sisters it is important that you balance
detachment and compassion.
It is to be in that place of support, open heartedness
and unconditional love; to show forth tenderness
and giving of yourself, without becoming hooked into the story;
without reinforcing feelings of victimhood or powerlessness.

now, my Beloved, that you have never made
a wrong decision or choice in your life.
Everything that you have ever done has brought you to this place,
this NOW of new knowledge, new choice-points and new opportunity.
You have never, nor will you ever, be judged
and condemned for anything you have done.
Everything is simply a learning experience for you to come to the
knowing that you are God-Goddess made manifest in this your
perceived reality; to come from separation to ONENESS
in this perfect and eternal NOW.

elf-honesty is a tool without which
you will find it very difficult to grow.
Without it, you find that you disguise and dress up
the reasons for your actions and reactions in order to feel
acceptable and worthy to yourself and others. By being honest
with yourself you have the most wonderful tool to discover your
secret fears and hidden beliefs about yourself and your reality.
In the embracement of those fears you become centered and strong.
This is called sovereignty, from whence come your creative choice
points to grow into your own power.

To be honest with others about who you are,
to speak your truth, is to be vulnerable.
Vulnerability is the most powerful place of being.
It is that place where there can be no dissension.
It is also the most fearful place for many of you, because you
fear judgement. You fear that if you open your heart,
someone will put a knife in it.
The reality is that when you speak forth your truth
you are really allowing the merging of hearts
to take place because vulnerability is irresistible.
When you find that there is truly nothing to defend, your ego
has taken a back seat and your heart is driving you
to a place of non-separation.

You ask about trust, Dear One.
Well, think about how you trust yourself. How much do you trust
that you are an eternal, unlimited Being who has the knowledge of the
multiverses within you?
How much do you trust that whatever experiences you bring forth
are opportunities for you to expand into the Light;
that the greater part of who you are, with the universe, supports
and nourishes you absolutely, if you will allow it?
When you trust your own Being
the question of trusting others does not arise.

ou ask: 'How can I trust?'
We say to you that you have unlimited trust, which you experience
every day of your life. You trust that the sun will rise each day.
Trust is what creates your reality.
Doubt is your trust that the outcome will be negative.
You may change that belief.

Honour who you are and in the doing you cannot but
honour every aspect of Creation.

What does that mean, really? It is simply that as you come to know
that who you are is a spark of Divine Creation you feel awe in the
wondrousness, immensity and power of you.

In the recognition of the pure potential of what it is to be a human
aspect of The All That Is, you are enflamed with love of you and able
to access that flame of Divinity not only within yourself but within
every unique aspect of Creation perceived in your reality.

You honour who you are by the allowance of BEING that unique
aspect of Creation that you are, without judgement. You honour all
life in the same way.

Laughter, Precious Being, that is the great aligner!
As you allow the joy and the laughter to bubble forth,
there is no judgement, no fear, no limited beliefs.
In those moments of great laughter you are truly in the NOW,
without past and without future, but simply in the eternal NOW, in
joy and alignment with your universe.
In that moment your brain releases the healing chemicals
which allow your body to reflect this unity in the manner
of health and well being.

The beauty which surrounds you is an exquisite mirror
for you to know how beautiful you really are.
When you acknowledge beauty it is to know that if you were not
beauty, how could you perceive it outside of you?
Do you judge the beauty of nature? No! It is all beautiful to you in a
myriad of different ways. You do not compare the beauty of a sunset
to the beauty of a blossom and say one is more beautiful than another.
In the same fashion do not compare yourself with any one else.
Each one of you is awesomely beauteous
in your own unique and divine fashion.
Without you, Beloved, the universes would not be the same.

From your belief structures about reality you see that everything
in your life is good-bad, positive-negative, happy and sad.
All of this dimension may be perceived as polarity.
However, be aware that polarity is an illusion.
What affects transformation is transcending that illusion of polarity.
Your beliefs may be likened unto the house that you live in,
which is very often a very tiny box which gives you no room to
stretch and grow. As you come to know that this illusion called life,
called polarity, called limitation, is self-imposed,
then by the simple act of choice you may transcend it,
to become limitless and sovereign.

ake time each day for yourself.
As you get caught up in the idea of 'duty', 'no time', 'must succeed',
and that anything which is pleasurable just for you must be selfish,
self-indulgent or not deserved, remind yourself that the very fact
that you exist makes you worthy of all the wondrousness
that you can imagine, and more.
By taking time each day for you to harmonize and balance yourself
you are honouring and nurturing yourself,
which enables you to be more creative, joyous and of greater service
to humanity in your day-to-day life.

*Beloved, we suggest to you that you learn to become
a creative detective, as in your books of fiction.
Only by learning the reasons for your re-active behavioural
patterns can you effect the changes that you desire in your life.
One of the maladies that besets you in your day-to-days
is what you term stress. What is stress? It is a manifestation of fear.
It is fear of an imagined outcome, which most often in your world
means failure. When you find yourself in stress or struggle,
be still and ask yourself:
'What am I afraid of here? What outcome am I attached to?'
You will be most surprised as you uncover beliefs that you did not
realize you held and which really no longer serve you.
Also, perhaps, how attached you are to what other people think of you.*

CHOICE!
You exercise it thousands of times each day without even realizing
you are doing so. Be aware of how you choose.
If you are going to do it, you might as well choose
joy and peace and harmony.

If you want to wait until everything is 'fixed'
before you will allow yourself to feel freedom and happiness,
be prepared for a short and miserable life! Do not wait.
Your freedom and happiness are a choice NOW.

verything in the world is valid,
else it would not exist. Everything has a purpose for the higher good.
Even that which you would judge to be most destructive upon your
plane may serve you, if you will allow it.

Keep it Simple.
Whatever the drama, whatever the story,
come back to the feeling.

*llow yourself to dream the impossible dream.
Allow your imagination to run wild.
Be who you are at this moment.
Thrill yourself with spontaneous action and be the child again.
Be practical. Plan for a miracle.
Ah! What excitement, Beloved.*

Being of service to others may be a smile,
a loving word or support when it is least expected.
Being of service to others is simply
to make a gift of who you are, to another.
BE the gift every day of your life.

*ear One, you are a miracle of this universe.
Acknowledge that you are, and look about you
to see the miracles reflected back to you. Allow the wonderment
of these miracles to permeate your being.
This wonderment is, indeed, life-renewing and life-affirming
and absolutely life-prolonging.*

No one and no-thing
can fill the empty space within you, except you.

As you are living in the focus of NOW,
without a past and without a future,
you are allowing the space for new knowledge
and solutions to 'problems' to float into your consciousness
without strife and struggle.

*here is no place on your Earth which is more sacred
than another. The place you are at this moment, on your Earth,
is where you are supposed to be, until the excitement or desire
of the heart will move you to another.
Know that you live in a safe universe.
No place is unsafe, really. Safety is within you, in the knowing that
you are safe. The universe supports that knowing absolutely.*

*You are more than your intelligence, more than your body,
more than your passions and more than your fears.
If you are ruled by any or more of these,
understand that it is a choice.
What is part of your soul energy is WILL.
You may choose to be the MORE of you and this WILL
and the universe, or God-Goddess energy, supports that choice.*

You have never made a wrong decision, my Beloved, and you never will. The effect of any decision is simply a learning experience, however you may judge it.

he macrocosmic universes
are what you may term the galaxies.
Microcosmic universes are contained within your own physical
structure. The mathematical dimensions are identical.
How is that for a miracle?

Freedom is knowing that in every moment
you have a choice.
Limitation is not exercising that choice.

The intellectual understanding of the concepts
we give forth to you are not enough to change your life, really.
However, by using that understanding to
RECOGNIZE THE FEELING,
to access your heart, will transform your life immediately.

*When something wondrous occurs in your life,
look in the mirror and say, 'I have created this.
I, this grand and multi-dimensional being, have created this.'*

Fourth density, transcendence, enlightenment,
or whatever you may call it,
is not issued forth as a panacea for the ills of your time.
It is simply the result of your embracement
of every facet of who you are.

s you focus on 'have not', you are not focusing on 'have'.
Whatever you focus on or put your energy into
is what you will draw to you.

ometimes you relate the idea of perfection to a
finished product and you perceive that when
you are perfect, you will be a 'finished' article, so to speak.
There is no finish, there is no end.
Who you are at this moment, in this now, is perfection
of the Mind of Creation, unto INFINITY.

In your world of polarity you are very concerned
with what you term 'profit and loss', 'win or lose'.
Know, however, that as you come into the knowing that you may
create whatever you desire, without 'need' or desperation, every
transaction may be one of win-win with profit to all, loss to none.

s you become more attuned, more in the knowing
that you are separate from nothing and no one,
you will find that the moments of illumination become longer
and longer, until there will be no time when you do not know
that you are truly an expression of the God-Goddess.

When you find yourself in a muddle, ask yourself:
'How would I deal with this if I were an enlightened one?'
Thusly you allow yourself to tap into the SELF of you who IS
an enlightened being and allow that knowing to issue forth.

*Vulnerability is one of the most powerful attributes.
Realize that if two people come together and one is vulnerable
there can be no confrontation. What is vulnerability?
It is to speak your truth, to open your heart and say:
'This is who I am and this is what frightens me.'*

When you find yourself struggling
to manipulate and control external events in your life,
look at the fear which lies beneath these actions.
If you would simply give up and allow the flow of events,
stating your preferred outcome, you would find that the result
will be exactly as you desired, without the struggle.

Love or fear - it is your choice in any moment
how you perceive it, how you live it.
You may cower in your fear or dance in the light.
The time will come when you will be very bored
with living in fear, being paralyzed in a no-life.
One day you will open your eyes and say:
'This day I will step into the Light.'

*very time you require a definition
you acquire a limitation.*

The changes which are occurring, heralding the
transition of the Earth and of humanity, need not be chaotic.
As you step further and further into the expansion of consciousness,
so you become more anchored in who you are. You will not be tossed
as a leaf in the wind, feeling powerless and out of control.
Rather you will be in joyous celebration of the changes,
garnering the wisdom and living in the Light of you.

hen you find yourself in defense
of people's opinions of you, it is your Ego defending itself.
When you say: 'But I...',
it is your Ego's defense mechanism kicking in. That is alright.
Embrace your Ego. It is frightened of being dispossessed.

*Imagine a string of light from your heart
connecting you to every other human upon your plane.
Now imagine many strings of light connecting you to every tree,
blade of grass, insect and animal.
From your crown, see a golden thread, which goes forth to the stars,
connecting you to every being on every planet of the universes
and all the dimensions.
Let that feeling resonate in your heart,
so you will know how it is to be in non-separation.*

You are loved and cherished on every dimension.
The names and numbers do not matter.
They do not mean anything to you. What is meaningful to you
is your own heart, your own soul, your own consciousness,
your own potential, your own divine beauty.
But we desire you to know that you are not alone.

Who you are is unlimited potential.
Who you are is a powerhouse, NOW.
Everything that has been in your past is who you are NOW.
It is alright. YOU are ALRIGHT.
You are everything you can possibly be at this moment.
You are glorious, and when you can accept that you are,
think of the tomorrows you will create!

nlightenment is not about being good.
It is about BEING.

What you invalidate, indeed, you empower.

s you label conscious, sub-conscious, un-conscious,
super-conscious, persona, body, spirit, soul and God,
you are compartmentalizing and separating
all the glorious parts of who you are.
That is alright, but know that you really are a homogenized body
of wondrous energy of Divinity experiencing
being human in this now.

When you can imagine the All-That-Is without personification, as such, then you may truly see the All-That-Is in everything, including who you are.

*That which you term 'religion' upon your plane
has nothing to do with the Spiritual truths of the universes,
which require no rites, rules or rituals.
Religion is a tool of enslavement to keep you in chains,
to keep you in control, that you may not know
sovereignty and free dominion.
It is valid. You have created it,
but it is not necessary for your enlightenment.*

ear One, you are every facet of every being
ever to walk this planet, and more.
You create every lifetime to garner every human experience,
and it is all a grand illusion.

hatever you use as a power-tool,
crystals and such like, are valid.
However, know that you are your own power-sourceness
and you need no outside tools for your inside enlightenment.

*Every situation has within it a pearl of wisdom,
if you will allow it. To harvest the pearls is to adorn yourself with
celestial jewels, to drape yourself in robes of celestial light, and to
grow wings with which to fly into the arms of eternal bliss.*

Until you can embrace and enjoy
all the facets of who you are, you are not whole.
When you are whole, it is called coming home.
There are wondrous beings who love you absolutely, who have
planned a glorious surprise party in celebration of your return!

There is no such thing as death.
When you become tired of wearing one colour every day of your life,
it is a joy to take off that suit of clothing.
Your body, you may say, is a suit of clothing.
When you take off that clothing
you do not cease to be the wondrous jewel you are.

*Sometimes when you are in a muddle,
you ask of the universe:
'Please send forth an answer to me,'
and you sit and wait to hear celestial voices.
Well, most often the answer is not in the form of a celestial voice,
but in something quite mundane in your day-to-day life.
If you are aware, you will see that you have created the answer in
the most tangible and irrefutable fashion.
When you have the expectation that the answers
may only occur in such and such way, you have closed down
all other possibilities for wisdom.*

Know that in the appearance of more war,
more violence and more discord you are seeing the polarity
of more love, more joy, more harmony.
The Love will embrace the fear and create Light.
As it is within you, so it is without.

This life is about BEING, human BEING,
however it is, with all its joys and all its sorrows.
Feel how exquisite it is, your tempestuous path to enlightenment.
You chose it. You love it.
If you did not, it would not be and that is the wondrous
and very humorous dichotomy of it.

When we speak of being as of 'higher dimension',
we speak of the rate of vibratory frequency, not as 'better than' or
'more important' than humanity.
There is no being anywhere who is more than another.
The angel is not more than the human.
The angel simply knows the 'MORE' of who it is.
You are still learning.
There is no hierarchy within Divinity.

You are a sexual being, from your birthing
to your transition, however you may express it.
When you look at how sex is used as a tool of manipulation
and embrace your fears around your sexuality, then truly,
sexuality may indeed become a most joyous expression of the heart,
an integrated facet of your own God-Goddessness.
Your sexual expression is no different than any other
outward expression of who you are.

Every action, every decision you have ever made
has brought you to this place, this now.
Bless every discordant circumstance
which has occurred in your life. You have created it all
that you may know who you really are.
Own it all. You are not a victim, and neither is anyone else.

hen you embrace all the things about yourself
which you find unlovable, you will have automatically allowed
the space for its opposite trait to manifest.

f you find yourself impatient and cross
because something you fervently desired is not made manifest,
be still and check any fear, belief, or expectation
which may be impeding the manifestation.
If you feel clear about that, then simply know
that the greater part of who you are has something much grander
lined up for you in the ripeness of time
than what you have envisioned. Allow it.

It is impossible to change
the expression of Divinity that you are.
You may simply acknowledge who you are, or not.
That is your choice.

Life is what is occurring
whilst you are very busy planning
your future and regretting your past.

Whatever you desire to manifest, simply put it forth
to the universe and KNOW that it already IS.
The moment you decide that what you desire can only occur
'this way', or in 'this timing', you are shutting down your own
creativity and millions of possibilities.
It is wonderful to make plans, but it is not to be rigid.
It is to allow the flow of creativity, that everything
may flow from your own Divinity, indeed.

*Doubt is of the intellect.
Knowing is of feeling.
If there is doubt, there is not knowing.
Knowing contains no doubt at all.*

When your hearts are quickened with excitement
and joy, every cell in your body resonates to that.
The cellular structure of your body, every cell,
EVERY cell, has its own consciousness, its own integrity,
its own joyous impetus of creativity.
In this fashion diseasement is not something you catch,
like a stray dog. The diseasement of your body, indeed,
is a reflection of the diseasement of your heart.

Each time, by word or deed, you invalidate yourself you will create situations which support that invalidation.

ou are so afraid to feel your feelings,
in the belief that you will die of the pain of it.
The truth is you will die if you do NOT go to the feeling.

For eons of time mankind has been living a dream
called reality.
It is your destiny to awaken from the dream
into the REALITY of DIVINITY.
Now is the time.

hose who would control you are those
who are afraid of not being in control.
Those who lust after power are those
who fear powerlessness.
Those who would steal are in fear of lack.
Those who would torment and torture are those
who, indeed, are tortured and tormented.
Beloved, have compassion for their fear.
As you may, without judgement, enfold these ones
into your heart, indeed you will change the reality.

*You may create the transition as you would desire it:
with love and joy and exuberance, in wild creativity,
with great honour and integrity.
The words you have will not describe the ecstatic explosion,
nor can you imagine how you will all be in that time,
when every atom and molecule upon this planet,
and the whole planet herself, will radiate with Divine Light.
Such exquisite beauty is beyond imaginings.*

The external situations in your life
have no meaning in and of themselves.
It is you, your consciousness, which designates a meaning.
If you designate a negative meaning, the result is negative.
By designating a positive meaning, the result is positive,
thusly allowing for expansion.

ou think that when you come into enlightenment
it is the end of it all. It is only the beginning.

The Self that you really are is more
than your waking or sleeping self, more than the emotions
you experience in your day-to-days.
The next time you are angry, be still and ask yourself,
'Who is angry?' The next time you are frustrated, or unhappy,
be still and ask yourself, 'Who is frustrated?', 'Who is unhappy?'
Just be still and listen. Feel the SELF of you.
This SELF is not angry, frustrated or unhappy.

Each time you invalidate anybody else,
you are invalidating who you are. As you invalidate yourself,
you are not allowing yourself to be who you are.
In this you disallow your own potential for expansion.

ou are the orchestrator of your own life.
You are the composer and the conductor
and all of the instruments in this grand orchestra.
You may create wonderful, wonderful symphonies.
We suggest that you become fascinated with the beauteous music
you create, that all of your life you may bring forth
the harmony of it.

In the changes which are occurring upon your planet
and in the transitions to come, there are many of humanity,
among what you would term to be the power brokers of your world,
who are plotting their own power-base.
In truth, they are working very well to accomplish that
which is completely unbeknown to them.
It is called 'God moves in mysterious ways', indeed.

our soul has no gender. It is not even human.
Allow yourself to contemplate this, in all its non-limitation.

What you regard as something very important
in your life and to which you devote much energy to create
takes no more energy than that which you regard to be quite
insignificant and create without thinking about it.
Is this food for thought?

ou cannot change what you do not acknowledge.
Acknowledge the beliefs and fears and self-invalidations
which keep you from the truth of who you really are.

Everything in physical existence is simply
coalesced energy which vibrates at its own frequency.
You have your own unique frequency, different to anyone else.
The frequency of humanity is different to the frequency
of a cow or a piece of furniture.
It is by these frequencies that you perceive differentiation.
In truth, energy is energy, and energy is of the Source.

There is nothing to do, nothing to fix.
It is simply to allow your Self to be excited by the idea
that you exist in this reality enveloped in the tender arms of the
Perfect and Divine Self of you, who is simply an extension of the
SOURCE.

Dear One, we ask you to contemplate this:
Love which is ego-based has somewhat of a feeling of fear,
or even entrapment, attached to it.
Love in the real sense has no thought of giving or receiving attached
to it at all. Love simply extends itself,
unmindful of anything else. Love simply IS.
Love is also simply who you really are.

The state of health or diseasement of your physical body
is simply a mirror of your emotional state of Being.
One is as valid as the other.
The universe does not judge one as being better or worse
than the other. Your body's desire at cellular level is to show forth
radiant wholeness, and as you heal and align your emotional body,
so your physical body will automatically reflect that change.

llow the children of your world to grow
with the knowledge of their own power,
that they create their own reality,
and allow them to know how to do that.
Allow them to know there is no such thing as 'success versus failure'.
Encourage their dreams, and tell them that by their dreams
and their imagination they create what they desire.
Teach them co-operative play rather than competition.
Honour their sovereignty and love them absolutely in the knowledge
they are Gods and Goddesses come forth
to be your teachers and mirrors.

If you were to stand aside from what you term to be your 'real life', you would know that in a manner of speaking your 'dream life' is more real than your waking reality. In your dream state you commune with other aspects of you, with dear friends and companions not of this reality, and indeed, those who are. Oftentimes you play and adventure in other dimensions and with beings you would regard to be extra-terrestrial. Understand that these communications are initiated by you, for your own expansion, even when you cannot bring forth any conscious remembrance. If you would desire to remember, simply ask forth before you sleep. However, know that many of these journeyings do not fit into the limited boxes of your definition of reality.

ou have control of your life
by letting go the NEED to control it.
Let go, and let GOD I AM.

*Y*ou are ALREADY the fourth density being
you desire to be.
You are ALREADY tapping into that higher consciousness
you think is so elusive.
You are ALREADY growing into the expansion
of who you really are.
As you believe it, so it is.
You are what you believe you are.

In the measure of basing your feelings of love, joy,
validation and success on other people and external events,
you are bound to feel rejection, unhappiness,
invalidation and failure.

There has existed and still does, in a fashion,
a belief that your bodies may be taken over
by what is termed to be 'evil spirits'.
We remind you that you are sovereign beings and not ever victims.
That which is termed evil is merely the manifestation of fear,
unembraced.

What you regard to be senility
is the gradual relinquishing of the present
and the desire to be gone from this place and time.
This signifies the loosening of the ties between consciousness and body
and the consciousness spending more and more time out of the body
to experience adventures of another kind.

Hating conflict and violence
will not bring harmony and peace.
Loving harmony and peace
brings harmony and peace.

Love is who you are.
Love is the true description of your SELF
as the thought of the Mind of Creation.
All else is an illusion, a misperception of the limited
ego-consciousness.

It is not that external events are your lessons.
Wisdom comes from the recognition of the
FEELINGS attached to those events.
The experiences you bring to yourself are often unpleasant
or discordant. This is simply your mind-set of eons of time
which tells you that as a guilty and unworthy person,
you deserve nothing better.

Look at how often each day
you turn your focus to what you perceive to be
the differences and conflicts within yourself
and between you and your brothers and sisters.
When you will turn your focus to unity,
to the exemplification of Divinity that you share,
then you will close that perceived gap called separation.

*he desire to manifest,
which comes out of a place of fear or need,
does not support the most fervent desire of your heart,
which is to come to know the God I Am,
who needs nothing and may have anything,
simply for the joy of it.*

We give forth words to you, and in a way,
these words create separation.
Your logical mind interprets the words according
to your own limited perceptions, fears and beliefs.
We would ask you to go to the feeling the words generate within you.
Thereby you may know their truth.

It is not necessary to go back into the past
to align what has created pain and anguish,
or indeed, to create the healing of your physical body.
It is only necessary in this now moment to embrace the thought
that you are a Divine and Perfect Expression of Creation.
In that thought you are automatically in that place of responsibility,
non-judgement and allowance of the feeling
which that thought engenders.

ther people's ideas
of who you are and who you should be
usually have nothing to do with the Truth of your Being.
You can buy into the limitation of these ideas or not.

There has always been somewhat of a fear within you
of the unknown quality of limitlessness,
of having no boundaries, of being infinite.
However, we assure you that just as you have already expanded
into your present state, which has now become quite familiar to you,
so it will continue in this fashion.
You truly have no limit and the Self of you
is very comfortable with its own infinite Divinity.

Beloved, we ask you to look
at how you all identify with roles.
The role of son or daughter, mother or father,
husband or wife, employer or employee.
Understand how you limit yourself by these ideas.
It is time now to step beyond the roles that have been
assigned to you and those you have assigned
to other people in your life.
Be aware of how your ideas of these roles
limit your relationships and keep you in chains.

eloved One,
the process of 'becoming' enlightened
is really a concept of ego-consciousness.
The truth is you are already
as perfect and Divine as you ever will be.
It is simply that this fact is not recognized
by the ego consciousness.
Will you remind yourself of this when you fall
into the dismals about your 'progress'?

s you allow yourself to reveal who you are
to those about you, so this allowance
will help heal the wounds of your heart.
As you reveal yourself, so the judgements and fears
about yourself are on the way to being aligned.
You only fear revelation because you secretly fear
you are less than you should be and that the real you
is absolutely unlovable.
How strange it is that all of the secret fears
of humanity are exactly the same!

Beloved, the Truth of how you may manifest
joy and harmony and abundance in your life is simple.
However, as you get caught up in the seeming complexity
of your day-to-day life, be aware that it is your mind-set
which creates the complexity.
You have a choice to continue in this mind-set or to be still
and look at HOW you create it and HOW you may change it.

In this timing in your society
many of you are feeling the stirring to do something different,
to change the pattern of your life.
Most of you have been programmed to think that once you have
made a choice as to what your 'life's work' is, then it would be
considered flighty or fickle to change it.
Also there enters in an element of fear around security.
We remind you that nothing is cast in stone, nor are any
of the multitudinous choices mutually exclusive.
It does not have to be 'this' or 'this' for the rest of your days.
It can be this AND this AND this AND this.
You really are grandly creative, Beloved.
You can do any thing you want. Go for it!
Follow your excitement!
Do what makes your heart sing!

It is most beneficial for you not to focus on what you
think must be 'fixed' before you can step into 'enlightenmen'.
There is nothing to fix and whatever you focus on you draw to you.
It is rather to focus on the joy of being God-Goddess
smelling the rose NOW.

The excitement and the singing of the heart, which you experience when you contemplate an imagined action, is the indication of the very real expression of who you are. When you deny the action, you deny yourself the gift of yourself to yourself and to your world.

Your life is not meant to be serious, my Beloved.
How long is it since you have allowed yourself light-heartedness
and laughter? All of this business is about enlightenment,
not enheavyment.

*You know, you really are so wonderful.
You are amazing, astonishingly beautiful and astonishingly courageous. We understand that most of the time you cannot acknowledge this to be so. However, Beloved, as you expand and reveal the YOU of you to yourself, you will see YOU with my eyes.
How is that for a tongue twister?
I salute you and love you absolutely.*

thank you for sharing who you are with that which be I.
As you are reading the words we have issued forth,
the essence of You mingles with the essence that I AM
in an ecstatic dance called Light, called Love.
We desire only to serve you, that you may recognize
the perfume of your own blossoming.

It is now time for you
to dwell in the House of eternal LOVE
and play in the garden called heaven
on the Earth of your own creation.
We are waiting for you.